G000244719

THE GOSPEL ACCORDING TO

MARK

with Introduction by

Henry Wansbrough OSB

*All booklets are published thanks to the
generous support of the members of the
Catholic Truth Society*

CATHOLIC TRUTH SOCIETY
PUBLISHERS TO THE HOLY SEE

CONTENTS

The Jerusalem Bible translation

The Jerusalem Bible was first published in 1966. It was produced by a team of distinguished English scholars (including J.R.R. Tolkien), working under Alexander Jones. It made available for English readers the findings of the French *Bible de Jérusalem* published a decade earlier by the famous French biblical school in Jerusalem, the first Catholic Bible edition to incorporate all the advances of modern biblical study. The Jerusalem Bible was the first translation of the whole Bible into modern English, and as such has maintained its status as authorised for use in the liturgy.

❧ INTRODUCTION ❧

Setting the scene

The story of Jesus is set in a remote corner of the Roman Empire, on a corridor of land between sea and desert which had already been trampled for centuries by conquering armies of Babylon, Syria, and Egypt when Rome began to dominate the area half a century before the birth of Jesus. It was home to the stubborn race of Jews, who refused to follow the other peoples of this great empire by abandoning their God and their religious tradition to fall in with the worship and culture of the Greco-Roman gods. This tradition was focussed on Jerusalem, itself dominated by the fabulous Temple of Herod, for which Jerusalem was renowned among the Romans as 'far the most distinguished city of the East' *(Pliny, Historia Naturalis)*. The story of Jesus begins in the Galilean countryside, some 70 miles to the north, where he first proclaimed the Kingdom of God (Mk 1:15), the long-awaited deliverance of Israel. It reaches its climax in Jerusalem, when Jesus confronts the authorities in the heartland of Judaism with his message (11:15-19), only to be rejected and executed with the connivance of the Roman governor (15:1-15). That is not the conclusion of the story, for Mark deliberately leaves his gospel suggestively open-ended (16:8).

The Good News of Jesus Christ

The overwhelming majority of scholars agree that the gospel according to Mark is the earliest of the three 'synoptic' gospels (so called because they share roughly the same outline, and so can be viewed concurrently at one glance) to be written down. Mark was chosen to put together a record of the stories which formed the Good News of Jesus Christ. He did not write a biography of Jesus in the modern sense, for he leaves out many details which would be fascinating to a modern reader, the appearance of Jesus, his childhood, his psychological development. He chooses and presents the incidents in order to convey the message of Jesus Christ, son of God.

Mark the evangelist

Who Mark was we do not know, and there is little reason to link him to any of the other people so named in the New Testament. 'Mark' was, after all, one of the commonest names in the Roman world. There is no suggestion that he was ever a companion of Jesus. Rather he assembled the stories that he received from the tradition. He may well have been a catechist who used the stories about Jesus in his own instruction, and his style betrays many of the features of oral story-telling. He is a master story-teller, with an eye for visual detail. He 'zooms in' on one memorable detail, like Jesus 'asleep in the boat, his head on the cushion' (4:38), or John the

4

Baptist's severed head on a dish (6:28). His language is simple and direct, the rough style of Greek which would have been used by ordinary people all around the eastern mediterranean. It has been described as 'kitchen Greek'. Many of the stories and sayings even hold traces of the Aramaic language in which Jesus himself will have spoken and in which the stories will originally have been told. But there is a uniform style throughout the gospel, which leaves no doubt that Mark was a real author.

At the same time, we can often tell from the emphasis placed on the stories that they will have been told and re-told in the earliest Christian communities to provide answers to questions: should we fast as the Jews do (2:18-20)? Should we observe the Jewish laws about clean and unclean food (7:14-23)? What will happen to those who are persecuted for following the way of Jesus (8:34-35)? Did Jesus know that such persecution would occur (13:9-13)? From the attitude to Judaism shown in the gospel, and from the limited knowledge of it presupposed (e.g. 7:11), we may deduce that Mark was writing for gentile Christians. Some early writers link Mark to Peter and even to Rome, but there can be little certainty about this. Nor can we know the date, for it is even unclear whether Mark is writing before or after the destruction of Jerusalem in AD 70; conventionally, therefore, the gospel is placed shortly before or after that event.

With this simple style Mark combines a brilliantly artistic pattern of arrangement, not necessarily in chronological order, but often grouping incidents of the same kind. So he gives a sample day of Jesus' activity on a Sabbath day in Capernaum (1:21-34), or assembles a group of Jesus' parables together (4:1-34). He balances a collection of controversies between Jesus and the Jewish authorities in Galilee early in his ministry (2:1-3.6) with another such collection of controversies with the Jewish authorities at Jerusalem in the final stages of his ministry there (12:1-40). Even the final week in Jerusalem may result from Mark's arrangement, for John depicts four different visits to Jerusalem.

Mark often 'sandwiches' a story between two other stories to bring out its meaning. He 'sandwiches' the story of the cleansing of the Temple between Jesus' curse on the fig-tree and the return of Jesus and the disciples to find the fig-tree withered (11:12-21). This is to hint that the worship conducted in the Temple was corrupt - the fig-tree of Israel was withered. The positioning of events is often symbolic: after the disciples have consistently failed to realise who Jesus is, we hear the story of the cure of the blind man at Bethsaida (8:22-26), and immediately afterwards Peter's eyes are opened and he acknowledges Jesus as the Messiah (8:29). Mark uses the fact that the Christian audience of the Gospel knows more than the actors in the story to create irony: the soldiers mock Jesus as King of Israel (15:18), when all the time we know that this is just what he was. James and John perkily ask for a position on Jesus' left and right (10:35-40), not knowing that Jesus is soon to be crucified between the two thieves who share his crucifixion.

Such irony is helped by the whole pattern of the gospel. It begins with an introduction which proclaims to the reader who Jesus is, messiah and son of God. Then the first disciples are called (1:16-20) and begin slowly, so slowly, to learn who Jesus is. The turning-point comes at Caesarea Philippi, when Peter sees that he is the Messiah. But Peter still does not realise what this implies. Three times Jesus prophesies that he must suffer and die (8:31; 9:31; 10:32-34), but each time the disciples fail to receive the message (8:32; 9:32-34; 10:35-40), and Jesus needs to explain again and again that his disciples must join him in service and suffering (8:34-38; 9:35-37; 10:41-45). Not until Jesus has died on the Cross does any human being proclaim him as son of God (15:39). This human being is a gentile centurion. During his life the gospel describes only one meeting between Jesus and a gentile. She wins his help almost against his will by her courageous and cheeky response (7:28). The centurion's acknowledgement is surely a symbol that at this moment the opening of the Good News to the gentiles begins.

The mystery of Jesus

Thus the whole gospel is centred on the mystery of Jesus. Jesus himself accepts none of the conventional titles offered to him, like Messiah (8:30), son of David (12:35-37), Lord (10:51). No ready-made formula suffices: he refers to himself by the mysterious, unexplained expression 'son of man'. Does this merely mean 'human being', or is Jesus alluding to the 'son of man' in the Book of Daniel (Dn 7:13), who receives all power on earth from the Ancient of Days? Mark certainly understands the expression in this sense, as we see at the trial scene before the High Priest (14:61-62). Before then we watch as Jesus calls his first four disciples; they follow in bewilderment this unknown charismatic figure (1:16-20). The amazement gradually grows as Jesus heals a sick man. Then he preaches with authority, not like the scribes and Pharisees, and they have to bow to his authority (1:21-28). He forgives sins as only God can do, and demonstrates his forgiveness with another cure (2:1-12). He interprets God's Law, the Law given to Moses, with the same awesomely authoritative voice (2:27-28). Then he silences the wind and the storm and passes over the backs of the waves, as only God can do (6:45-52). And all the time he is proclaiming that the Kingship or Sovereignty of God has come into the world in a new way, backing up his proclamation by wiping away the horrors of sickness and death, welcoming outcasts and sinners to forgiveness (2:15-17). The unclean spirits from whom he liberates the tormented sufferers cannot fail to acknowledge that God is at work in Jesus (1:24; 5:7), an acknowledgement which still leaves the human onlookers awed but puzzled. Even when Peter realises that he is the final messenger from God, the disciples three times fail to understand his predictions of suffering, three times let him down in Gethsemane and eventually run away (14:32-50). At the beginning they left all to follow him, and now the young man leaves all to run away naked (14:51-52)! Three times Peter denies knowledge of Jesus, just at the moment when Jesus is making his fullest claim to divine status before the High Priest (14:54-72). It is left to Pilate three times to declare his innocence (15:1-15) and to the centurion to declare that he is son of God. Even at the explosive final scene of the Empty Tomb (the last few verses after 16:8 form a later addition) the faithful women are merely terrified at the news that Jesus has risen from the dead, and flee uncomprehending, silent in their fear.

The failure of the disciples

Scholars have long puzzled why Mark placed such emphasis on the failure of the disciples. At first they respond enthusiastically, but soon Jesus begins to rebuke them sternly for their lack of understanding (4:40; 8:17-18). They, on their part, can be sarcastic towards their Master (5:31; 6:37). Their behaviour often contrasts unfavourably with that of others who encounter Jesus in the course of his ministry (7:26-30; 8:22-26). Is this to show that it is easy to come to Jesus, but harder to stick by him when difficulties arise (as in the parable of the Sower 4:3-8)? Or is it a warning that any deep appreciation of Jesus is difficult of itself? Or is Mark looking sideways at a group in his own community who have failed under persecution, but must be brought back and reconciled? Or is it merely a literary technique to enable Mark to progress from one story to another? In any case, this is one of the major emphases of Mark's presentation.

Reading Mark

The brevity, simplicity and vividness of Mark make this the easiest gospel to read straight through. Try reading it through as though you had never heard of Jesus before, and meet this personality and his message afresh! But also read it prayerfully and meditatively, remembering that it is the record of the Good News of God, given two thousand years ago to a particular group of people, but addressed as a message of salvation to the whole world.

The Gospel According to
❧ Mark ❧

I. Prelude to the Public Ministry of Jesus

The preaching of John the Baptist

1 [1]The beginning of the Good News about Jesus Christ, the Son of God. [2]It is written in the book of the prophet Isaiah:

Look, I am going to send my messenger before you;
he will prepare your way.
[3]*A voice cries in the wilderness:*
Prepare a way for the Lord, make his paths straight,[a]

[4]and so it was that John the Baptist appeared in the wilderness, proclaiming a baptism of repentance for the forgiveness of sins. [5]All Judaea and all the people of Jerusalem made their way to him, and as they were baptised by him in the river Jordan they confessed their sins. [6]John wore a garment of camel-skin, and he lived on locusts and wild honey. [7]In the course of his preaching he said, 'Someone is following me, someone who is more powerful than I am, and I am not fit to kneel down and undo the strap of his sandals. [8]I have baptised you with water, but he will baptise you with the Holy Spirit.'

Jesus is baptised

[9]It was at this time that Jesus came from Nazareth in Galilee and was baptised in the Jordan by John.

---

[1]a. Is 40:3

¹⁰No sooner had he come up out of the water than he saw the heavens torn apart and the Spirit, like a dove, descending on him. ¹¹And a voice came from heaven, 'You are my Son, the Beloved; my favour rests on you.'

Temptation in the wilderness

¹²Immediately afterwards the Spirit drove him out into the wilderness ¹³and he remained there for forty days, and was tempted by Satan. He was with the wild beasts, and the angels looked after him.

II. THE GALILEAN MINISTRY

Jesus begins to preach

¹⁴After John had been arrested, Jesus went into Galilee. There he proclaimed the Good News from God. ¹⁵'The time has come' he said 'and the kingdom of God is close at hand. Repent, and believe the Good News.'

The first four disciples are called

¹⁶As he was walking along by the Sea of Galilee he saw Simon and his brother Andrew casting a net in the lake - for they were fishermen. ¹⁷And Jesus said to them, 'Follow me and I will make you into fishers of men'.¹⁸And at once they left their nets and followed him. ¹⁹Going on a little further, he saw James son of Zebedee and his brother John; they too were in their boat, mending their nets. He called them at once ²⁰and, leaving their father Zebedee in the boat with the men he employed, they went after him.

Jesus teaches in Capernaum and cures a demoniac

²¹They went as far as Capernaum, and as soon as the sabbath came he went to the synagogue and began to teach. ²²And his teaching made a deep impression on them because, unlike the scribes, he taught them with authority. ²³In their synagogue just then there was a man possessed by an unclean spirit and it shouted, ²⁴'What do you want with us, Jesus of Nazareth? Have you come to destroy us? I know who you are: the Holy One of God.' ²⁵But Jesus said sharply, 'Be quiet! Come out of him!' ²⁶And the unclean spirit threw the man into convulsions and with a loud cry went out of him. ²⁷The people were so astonished that they started asking each other what it all meant. 'Here is a teaching that is new' they said 'and with authority behind it: he gives orders even to unclean spirits and they obey him.' ²⁸And his reputation rapidly spread everywhere, through all the surrounding Galilean countryside.

Cure of Simon's mother-in-law

²⁹On leaving the synagogue, he went with James and John straight to the house of Simon and Andrew. ³⁰Now Simon's mother-in-law had gone to bed with fever, and they told him about her straightaway. ³¹He went to her, took her by the hand and helped her up. And the fever left her and she began to wait on them.

A number of cures

³²That evening, after sunset, they brought to him all who were sick and those who were possessed by devils.

13

[33]The whole town came crowding round the door, [34]and he cured many who were suffering from diseases of one kind or another; he also cast out many devils, but he would not allow them to speak, because they knew who he was.[b]

Jesus quietly leaves Capernaum and travels through Galilee

[35]In the morning, long before dawn, he got up and left the house, and went off to a lonely place and prayed there. [36]Simon and his companions set out in search of him, [37]and when they found him they said, 'Everybody is looking for you'. [38]He answered, 'Let us go elsewhere, to the neighbouring country towns, so that I can preach there too, because that is why I came'. [39]And he went all through Galilee, preaching in their synagogues and casting out devils.

Cure of a leper

[40]A leper came to him and pleaded on his knees: 'If you want to' he said 'you can cure me'. [41]Feeling sorry for him, Jesus stretched out his hand and touched him. 'Of course I want to!' he said. 'Be cured!' [42]And the leprosy left him at once and he was cured. [43]Jesus immediately sent him away and sternly ordered him, [44]'Mind you say nothing to anyone, but go and show yourself to the priest, and make the offering for your healing prescribed by Moses as

---

[1 b.] Throughout this gospel, Jesus never explicitly claims to be the Messiah and he forbids others to speak of the fact.

evidence of your recovery'. [45]The man went away, but then started talking about it freely and telling the story everywhere, so that Jesus could no longer go openly into any town, but had to stay outside in places where nobody lived. Even so, people from all around would come to him.

Cure of a paralytic

2 [1]When he returned to Capernaum some time later, word went round that he was back; [2]and so many people collected that there was no room left, even in front of the door. He was preaching the word to them [3]when some people came bringing him a paralytic carried by four men, [4]but as the crowd made it impossible to get the man to him, they stripped the roof over the place where Jesus was; and when they had made an opening, they lowered the stretcher on which the paralytic lay. [5]Seeing their faith, Jesus said to the paralytic, 'My child, your sins are forgiven'. [6]Now some scribes were sitting there, and they thought to themselves, [7]'How can this man talk like that? He is blaspheming. Who can forgive sins but God?' [8]Jesus, inwardly aware that this was what they were thinking, said to them, 'Why do you have these thoughts in your hearts? [9]Which of these is easier: to say to the paralytic, "Your sins are forgiven" or to say, "Get up, pick up your stretcher and walk"? [10]But to prove to you that the Son of Man has authority on earth to forgive sins,' - [11]he said to the paralytic - 'I order you: get up, pick

up your stretcher, and go off home.' [12]And the man got up, picked up his stretcher at once and walked out in front of everyone, so that they were all astounded and praised God saying, 'We have never seen anything like this'.

The call of Levi

[13]He went out again to the shore of the lake;[a] and all the people came to him, and he taught them. [14]As he was walking on he saw Levi the son of Alphaeus, sitting by the customs house, and he said to him, 'Follow me'. And he got up and followed him.

Eating with sinners

[15]When Jesus was at dinner in his house, a number of tax collectors and sinners were also sitting at the table with Jesus and his disciples; for there were many of them among his followers. [16]When the scribes of the Pharisee party saw him eating with sinners and tax collectors, they said to his disciples, 'Why does he eat with tax collectors and sinners?' [17]When Jesus heard this he said to them, 'It is not the healthy who need the doctor, but the sick. I did not come to call the virtuous, but sinners.'

A discussion on fasting

[18]One day when John's disciples and the Pharisees were fasting, some people came and said to him, 'Why is it that John's disciples and the disciples of the Pharisees fast,

---

[2a.] Tiberias, the 'Sea of Galilee'.

but your disciples do not?' [19]Jesus replied, 'Surely the bridegroom's attendants would never think of fasting while the bridegroom is still with them? As long as they have the bridegroom with them, they could not think of fasting. [20]But the time will come for the bridegroom to be taken away from them, and then, on that day, they will fast. [21]No one sews a piece of unshrunken cloth on an old cloak; if he does, the patch pulls away from it, the new from the old, and the tear gets worse. [22]And nobody puts new wine into old wineskins; if he does, the wine will burst the skins, and the wine is lost and the skins too. No! New wine, fresh skins!'

Picking corn on the Sabbath

[23]One sabbath day he happened to be taking a walk through the cornfields, and his disciples began to pick ears of corn as they went along. [24]And the Pharisees said to him, 'Look, why are they doing something on the sabbath day that is forbidden?' [25]And he replied, 'Did you never read what David did in his time of need when he and his followers were hungry - [26]how he went into the house of God when Abiathar[b] was high priest, and ate the loaves of offering which only the priests are allowed to eat, and how he also gave some to the men with him?' [27]And he said to them, 'The sabbath was made for man,

---

[2b.] See 1 S 21:1-7. Abiathar was the better known as high priest in David's reign, but Ahimelech is named in this source.

not man for the sabbath; [28]the Son of Man is master even of the sabbath'.

Cure of the man with a withered hand

3 [1]He went again into a synagogue, and there was a man there who had a withered hand. [2]And they were watching him to see if he would cure him on the sabbath day, hoping for something to use against him. [3]He said to the man with the withered hand, 'Stand up out in the middle!' [4]Then he said to them, 'Is it against the law on the sabbath day to do good, or to do evil; to save life, or to kill?' But they said nothing. [5]Then, grieved to find them so obstinate, he looked angrily round at them, and said to the man, 'Stretch out your hand'. He stretched it out and his hand was better. [6]The Pharisees went out and at once began to plot with the Herodians against him, discussing how to destroy him.

The crowds follow Jesus

[7]Jesus withdrew with his disciples to the lakeside, and great crowds from Galilee followed him. From Judaea, [8]Jerusalem, Idumaea, Transjordania and the region of Tyre and Sidon, great numbers who had heard of all he was doing came to him. [9]And he asked his disciples to have a boat ready for him because of the crowd, to keep him from being crushed. [10]For he had cured so many that all who were afflicted in any way were crowding forward to touch him. [11]And the unclean spirits, whenever they saw him, would fall

down before him and shout, 'You are the Son of God!' [12]But he warned them strongly not to make him known.

The appointment of the Twelve

[13]He now went up into the hills and summoned those he wanted. So they came to him [14]and he appointed twelve; they were to be his companions and to be sent out to preach, [15]with power to cast out devils. [16]And so he appointed the Twelve: Simon to whom he gave the name Peter, [17]James the son of Zebedee and John the brother of James, to whom he gave the name Boanerges or 'Sons of Thunder'; [18]then Andrew, Philip, Bartholomew, Matthew, Thomas, James the son of Alphaeus, Thaddaeus, Simon the Zealot [19]and Judas Iscariot, the man who was to betray him.

His relatives are concerned about Jesus

[20]He went home again, and once more such a crowd collected that they could not even have a meal. [21]When his relatives heard of this, they set out to take charge of him, convinced he was out of his mind.

Allegations of the scribes

[22]The scribes who had come down from Jerusalem were saying, 'Beelzebul is in him' and, 'It is through the prince of devils that he casts devils out'. [23]So he called them to him and spoke to them in parables, 'How can Satan cast out Satan? [24]If a kingdom is divided against itself, that kingdom cannot last. [25]And if a household is

divided against itself, that household can never stand.
²⁶Now if Satan has rebelled against himself and is
divided, he cannot stand either - it is the end of him.
²⁷But no one can make his way into a strong man's
house and burgle his property unless he has tied up the
strong man first. Only then can he burgle his house. ²⁸I
tell you solemnly, all men's sins will be forgiven, and
all their blasphemies; ²⁹but let anyone blaspheme against
the Holy Spirit and he will never have forgiveness: he is
guilty of an eternal sin.' ³⁰This was because they were
saying, 'An unclean spirit is in him'.

The true kinsmen of Jesus
³¹His mother and brothers now arrived and, standing
outside, sent in a message asking for him. ³²A crowd was
sitting round him at the time the message was passed to
him, 'Your mother and brothers and sisters are outside
asking for you'. ³³He replied, 'Who are my mother and
my brothers?' ³⁴And looking round at those sitting in a
circle about him, he said, 'Here are my mother and my
brothers. ³⁵Anyone who does the will of God, that person
is my brother and sister and mother.'

Parable of the sower
4 ¹Again he began to teach by the lakeside, but such a
huge crowd gathered round him that he got into a boat
on the lake and sat there. The people were all along the
shore, at the water's edge. ²He taught them many things

in parables, and in the course of his teaching he said to them, [3]'Listen! Imagine a sower going out to sow. [4]Now it happened that, as he sowed, some of the seed fell on the edge of the path, and the birds came and ate it up. [5]Some seed fell on rocky ground where it found little soil and sprang up straightaway, because there was no depth of earth; [6]and when the sun came up it was scorched and, not having any roots, it withered away. [7]Some seed fell into thorns, and the thorns grew up and choked it, and it produced no crop. [8]And some seeds fell into rich soil and, growing tall and strong, produced crop; and yielded thirty, sixty, even a hundredfold.' [9]And he said, 'Listen, anyone who has ears to hear!'

Why Jesus speaks in parables
[10]When he was alone, the Twelve, together with the others who formed his company, asked what the parables meant. [11]He told them, 'The secret of the kingdom of God is given to you, but to those who are outside everything comes in parables, [12]so that *they may see and see again, but not perceive; may hear and hear again, but not understand; otherwise they might be converted and be forgiven'.*[a]

The parable of the sower explained
[13]He said to them, 'Do you not understand this parable? Then how will you understand any of the parables? [14]What the sower is sowing is the word. [15]Those on the edge of the

---

[4a.] Is 6:9-10

21

path where the word is sown are people who have no sooner heard it than Satan comes and carries away the word that was sown in them. [16]Similarly, those who receive the seed on patches of rock are people who, when first they hear the word, welcome it at once with joy. [17]But they have no root in them, they do not last; should some trial come, or some persecution on account of the word, they fall away at once. [18]Then there are others who receive the seed in thorns. These have heard the word, [19]but the worries of this world, the lure of riches and all the other passions come in to choke the word, and so it produces nothing. [20]And there are those who have received the seed in rich soil: they hear the word and accept it and yield a harvest, thirty and sixty and a hundredfold.'

Parable of the lamp

[21]He also said to them, 'Would you bring in a lamp to put it under a tub or under the bed? Surely you will put it on the lamp-stand? [22]For there is nothing hidden but it must be disclosed, nothing kept secret except to be brought to light. [23]If anyone has ears to hear, let him listen to this.'

Parable of the measure

[24]He also said to them, 'Take notice of what you are hearing. The amount you measure out is the amount you will be given - and more besides; [25]for the man who has will be given more; from the man who has not, even what he has will be taken away.'

Parable of the seed growing by itself

[26]He also said, 'This is what the kingdom of God is like. A man throws seed on the land. [27]Night and day, while he sleeps, when he is awake, the seed is sprouting and growing; how, he does not know. [28]Of its own accord the land produces first the shoot, then the ear, then the full grain in the ear. [29]And when the crop is ready, he loses no time: he starts to reap because the harvest has come.'

Parable of the mustard seed

[30]He also said, 'What can we say the kingdom of God is like? What parable can we find for it? [31]It is like a mustard seed which at the time of its sowing in the soil is the smallest of all the seeds on earth; [32]yet once it is sown it grows into the biggest shrub of them all and puts out big branches so that the birds of the air can shelter in its shade.'

The use of parables

[33]Using many parables like these, he spoke the word to them, so far as they were capable of understanding it. [34]He would not speak to them except in parables, but he explained everything to his disciples when they were alone.

The calming of the storm

[35]With the coming of evening that same day, he said to them, 'Let us cross over to the other side'. [36]And leaving

the crowd behind they took him, just as he was, in the boat; and there were other boats with him. [37]Then it began to blow a gale and the waves were breaking into the boat so that it was almost swamped. [38]But he was in the stern, his head on the cushion, asleep. [39]They woke him and said to him, 'Master, do you not care? We are going down!' And he woke up and rebuked the wind and said to the sea, 'Quiet now! Be calm!' And the wind dropped, and all was calm again. [40]Then he said to them, 'Why are you so frightened? How is it that you have no faith?' [41]They were filled with awe and said to one another, 'Who can this be? Even the wind and the sea obey him.'

The Gerasene demoniac

5 [1]They reached the country of the Gerasenes[a] on the other side of the lake, [2]and no sooner had he left the boat than a man with an unclean spirit came out from the tombs towards him. [3]The man lived in the tombs and no one could secure him any more, even with a chain; [4]because he had often been secured with fetters and chains but had snapped the chains and broken the fetters, and no one had the strength to control him. [5]All night and all day, among the tombs and in the mountains, he would howl and gash himself with stones. [6]Catching sight of Jesus from a distance, he ran up and fell at his feet [7]and shouted at the top of his voice, 'What do you want with me, Jesus,

---

[5a]. 'Gadarenes' in some versions.

son of the Most High God? Swear by God you will not torture me!' [8]– For Jesus had been saying to him, 'Come out of the man, unclean spirit'. [9]'What is your name?' Jesus asked. 'My name is legion,' he answered 'for there are many of us.' [10]And he begged him earnestly not to send them out of the district. [11]Now there was there on the mountainside a great herd of pigs feeding, [12]and the unclean spirits begged him, 'Send us to the pigs, let us go into them'. [13]So he gave them leave. With that, the unclean spirits came out and went into the pigs, and the herd of about two thousand pigs charged down the cliff into the lake, and there they were drowned. [14]The swineherds ran off and told their story in the town and in the country round about; and the people came to see what had really happened. [15]They came to Jesus and saw the demoniac sitting there, clothed and in his full senses - the very man who had had the legion in him before - and they were afraid. [16]And those who had witnessed it reported what had happened to the demoniac and what had become of the pigs. [17]Then they began to implore Jesus to leave the neighbourhood. [18]As he was getting into the boat, the man who had been possessed begged to be allowed to stay with him. [19]Jesus would not let him but said to him, 'Go home to your people and tell them all that the Lord in his mercy has done for you'. [20]So the man went off and proceeded to spread throughout the Decapolis all that Jesus had done for him. And everyone was amazed.

Cure of the woman with a haemorrhage.
The daughter of Jairus raised to life

²¹When Jesus had crossed again in the boat to the other side, a large crowd gathered round him and he stayed by the lakeside. ²²Then one of the synagogue officials came up, Jairus by name, and seeing him, fell at his feet ²³and pleaded with him earnestly, saying, 'My little daughter is desperately sick. Do come and lay your hands on her to make her better and save her life.' ²⁴Jesus went with him and a large crowd followed him; they were pressing all round him. ²⁵Now there was a woman who had suffered from a haemorrhage for twelve years; ²⁶after long and painful treatment under various doctors, she spent all she had without being any the better for it, in fact, she was getting worse. ²⁷She had heard about Jesus, and she came up behind him through the crowd and touched his cloak. ²⁸'If I can touch even his clothes,' she had told herself 'I shall be well again.' ²⁹And the source of the bleeding dried up instantly, and she felt in herself that she was cured of her complaint. ³⁰Immediately aware that power had gone out from him, Jesus turned round in the crowd and said, 'Who touched my clothes?' ³¹His disciples said to him, 'You see how the crowd is pressing round you and yet you say, "Who touched me?"' ³²But he continued to look all round to see who had done it. ³³Then the woman came forward,

frightened and trembling[b] because she knew what had happened to her, and she fell at his feet and told him the whole truth. [34]'My daughter,' he said 'your faith has restored you to health; go in peace and be free from your complaint.' [35]While he was still speaking some people arrived from the house of the synagogue official to say, 'Your daughter is dead: why put the Master to any further trouble?' [36]But Jesus had overheard this remark of theirs and he said to the official, 'Do not be afraid; only have faith'. [37]And he allowed no one to go with him except Peter and James and John the brother of James. [38]So they came to the official's house and Jesus noticed all the commotion, with people weeping and wailing unrestrainedly. [39]He went in and said to them, 'Why all this commotion and crying? The child is not dead, but asleep.' [40]But they laughed at him. So he turned them all out and, taking with him the child's father and mother and his own companions, he went into the place where the child lay. [41]And taking the child by the hand he said to her, 'Talitha, kum!' which means, 'Little girl, I tell you to get up'. [42]The little girl got up at once and began to walk about, for she was twelve years old. At this they were overcome with astonishment, [43]and he ordered them strictly not to let anyone know about it, and told them to give her something to eat.

[5 b.] According to the Law, she was unclean, and to be touched by her would be defilement.

A visit to Nazareth

6 ¹Going from that district, he went to his home town and his disciples accompanied him. ²With the coming of the sabbath he began teaching in the synagogue and most of them were astonished when they heard him. They said, 'Where did the man get all this? What is this wisdom that has been granted him, and these miracles that are worked through him? ³This is the carpenter, surely, the son of Mary, the brother of James and Joset and Jude and Simon? His sisters, too, are they not here with us?' And they would not accept him. ⁴And Jesus said to them, 'A prophet is only despised in his own country, among his own relations and in his own house'; ⁵and he could work no miracle there, though he cured a few sick people by laying his hands on them. ⁶He was amazed at their lack of faith.

The mission of the Twelve

He made a tour round the villages, teaching. ⁷Then he summoned the Twelve and began to send them out in pairs giving them authority over the unclean spirits. ⁸And he instructed them to take nothing for the journey except a staff - no bread, no haversack, no coppers for their purses. ⁹They were to wear sandals but, he added, 'Do not take a spare tunic'. ¹⁰And he said to them, 'If you enter a house anywhere, stay there until you leave the district. ¹¹And if any place does not welcome you and people refuse to listen to you, as you walk away shake off the dust from under your feet as a sign to them.' ¹²So they set off to preach repentance; ¹³and they cast out many devils, and anointed many sick people with oil and cured them.

Herod and Jesus

¹⁴Meanwhile King Herod had heard about him, since by now his name was well-known. Some were saying, 'John the Baptist has risen from the dead, and that is why miraculous powers are at work in him'. ¹⁵Others said, 'He is Elijah'; others again, 'He is a prophet, like the prophets we used to have'. ¹⁶But when Herod heard this he said, 'It is John whose head I cut off; he has risen from the dead'.

John the Baptist beheaded

¹⁷Now it was this same Herod who had sent to have John arrested, and had him chained up in prison because of Herodias, his brother Philip's wife whom he had married. ¹⁸For John had told Herod, 'It is against the law for you to have your brother's wife'. ¹⁹As for Herodias, she was furious with him and wanted to kill him; but she was not able to, ²⁰because Herod was afraid of John, knowing him to be a good and holy man, and gave him his protection. When he had heard him speak he was greatly perplexed, and yet he liked to listen to him. ²¹An opportunity came on Herod's birthday when he gave a banquet for the nobles of his court, for his army officers and for the leading figures in Galilee. ²²When the daughter of this same Herodias came in and danced, she delighted Herod

and his guests; so the king said to the girl, 'Ask me anything you like and I will give it you'. ²³And he swore her an oath, 'I will give you anything you ask, even half my kingdom'. ²⁴She went out and said to her mother, 'What shall I ask for?' She replied, 'The head of John the Baptist' ²⁵The girl hurried straight back to the king and made her request, 'I want you to give me John the Baptist's head, here and now, on a dish'. ²⁶The king was deeply distressed but, thinking of the oaths he had sworn and of his guests, he was reluctant to break his word to her. ²⁷So the king at once sent one of the bodyguard with orders to bring John's head. ²⁸The man went off and beheaded him in prison; then he brought the head on a dish and gave it to the girl, and the girl gave it to her mother. ²⁹When John's disciples heard about this, they came and took his body and laid it in a tomb.

First miracle of the loaves

³⁰The apostles rejoined Jesus and told him all they had done and taught. ³¹Then he said to them, 'You must come away to some lonely place all by yourselves and rest for a while'; for there were so many coming and going that the apostles had no time even to eat. ³²So they went off in a boat to a lonely place where they could be by themselves. ³³But people saw them going, and many could guess where; and from every town they all hurried to the place on foot and reached it before them. ³⁴So as he stepped

ashore he saw a large crowd; and he took pity on them because they were like sheep without a shepherd, and he set himself to teach them at some length. ³⁵By now it was getting very late, and his disciples came up to him and said, 'This is a lonely place and it is getting very late, ³⁶so send them away, and they can go to the farms and villages round about, to buy themselves something to eat'. ³⁷He replied, 'Give them something to eat yourselves'. They answered, 'Are we to go and spend two hundred denarii on bread for them to eat?' ³⁸How many loaves have you?' he asked 'Go and see.' And when they had found out they said, 'Five, and two fish'. ³⁹Then he ordered them to get all the people together in groups on the green grass, ⁴⁰and they sat down on the ground in squares of hundreds and fifties. ⁴¹Then he took the five loaves and the two fish, raised his eyes to heaven and said the blessing; then he broke the loaves and handed them to his disciples to distribute among the people. He also shared out the two fish among them all. ⁴²They all ate as much as they wanted. ⁴³They collected twelve basketfuls of scraps of bread and pieces of fish. ⁴⁴Those who had eaten the loaves numbered five thousand men.

Jesus walks on the water

⁴⁵Directly after this he made his disciples get into the boat and go on ahead to Bethsaida, while he himself sent the crowd away. ⁴⁶After saying good-bye to them he went off

into the hills to pray. [47]When evening came, the boat was far out on the lake, and he was alone on the land. [48]He could see they were worn out with rowing, for the wind was against them; and about the fourth watch of the night he came towards them, walking on the lake. He was going to pass them by, [49]but when they saw him walking on the lake they thought it was a ghost and cried out; [50]for they had all seen him and were terrified. But he at once spoke to them, and said, 'Courage! It is I! Do not be afraid.' [51]Then he got into the boat with them, and the wind dropped. They were utterly and completely dumbfounded, [52]because they had not seen what the miracle of the loaves meant; their minds were closed.

Cures at Gennesaret

[53]Having made the crossing, they came to land at Gennesaret and tied up. [54]No sooner had they stepped out of the boat than people recognised him, [55]and started hurrying all through the countryside and brought the sick on stretchers to wherever they heard he was. [56]And wherever he went, to village, or town, or farm, they laid down the sick in the open spaces, begging him to let them touch even the fringe of his cloak. And all those who touched him were cured.

The traditions of the Pharisees

7 [1]The Pharisees and some of the scribes who had come from Jerusalem gathered round him, [2]and they noticed that some of his disciples were eating with unclean hands, that is,

without washing them. ³For the Pharisees, and the Jews in general, follow the tradition of the elders and never eat without washing their arms as far as the elbow; ⁴and on returning from the market place they never eat without first sprinkling themselves. There are also many other observances which have been handed down to them concerning the washing of cups and pots and bronze dishes. ⁵So these Pharisees and scribes asked him, 'Why do your disciples not respect the tradition of the elders but eat their food with unclean hands?' ⁶He answered, 'It was of you hypocrites that Isaiah so rightly prophesied in this passage of scripture:

This people honours me only with lip-service,
while their hearts are far from me.
⁷*The worship they offer me is worthless,*
*the doctrines they teach are only human regulations.*ᵃ

⁸You put aside the commandment of God to cling to human traditions.' ⁹And he said to them, 'How ingeniously you get round the commandment of God in order to preserve your own tradition! ¹⁰For Moses said: *Do your duty to your father and your mother*, and, *Anyone who curses father or mother must be put to death*. ¹¹But you say, "If a man says to his father or mother: Anything I have that I might have used to help you is Corbanᵇ (that is, dedicated to God), ¹²then he is forbidden from that moment to do anything for his father or mother". ¹³In this way you make God's word null and void

---

⁷ᵃ· Is 29:13
⁷ᵇ· See note on Mt 15:6

for the sake of your tradition which you have handed down. And you do many other things like this.'

On clean and unclean

[14]He called the people to him again and said, 'Listen to me, all of you, and understand. [15]Nothing that goes into a man from outside can make him unclean; it is the things that come out of a man that make him unclean. [16]If anyone has ears to hear, let him listen to this.' [17]When he had gone back into the house, away from the crowd, his disciples questioned him about the parable. [18]He said to them, 'Do you not understand either? Can you not see that whatever goes into a man from outside cannot make him unclean, [19]because it does not go into his heart but through his stomach and passes out into the sewer?' (Thus he pronounced all foods clean.) [20]And he went on, 'It is what comes out of a man that makes him unclean. [21]For it is from within, from men's hearts, that evil intentions emerge: fornication, theft, murder, adultery, [22]avarice, malice, deceit, indecency, envy, slander, pride, folly. [23]All these evil things come from within and make a man unclean.'

III. JOURNEYS OUTSIDE GALILEE

The daughter of the Syrophoenician woman healed

[24]He left that place and set out for the territory of Tyre. There he went into a house and did not want anyone to know he was there, but he could not pass unrecognised.

²⁵A woman whose little daughter had an unclean spirit heard about him straightaway and came and fell at his feet. ²⁶Now the woman was a pagan, by birth a Syrophoenician, and she begged him to cast the devil out of her daughter. ²⁷And he said to her, 'The children should be fed first, because it is not fair to take the children's food and throw it to the house-dogs'. ²⁸But she spoke up: 'Ah yes, sir,' she replied 'but the house-dogs under the table can eat the children's scraps'. ²⁹And he said to her, 'For saying this, you may go home happy: the devil has gone out of your daughter'. ³⁰So she went off to her home and found the child lying on the bed and the devil gone.

Healing of the deaf man

³¹Returning from the district of Tyre, he went by way of Sidon towards the Sea of Galilee, right through the Decapolis region. ³²And they brought him a deaf man who had an impediment in his speech; and they asked him to lay his hand on him. ³³He took him aside in private, away from the crowd, put his fingers into the man's ears and touched his tongue with spittle. ³⁴Then looking up to heaven he sighed; and he said to him, 'Ephphatha', that is, 'Be opened'. ³⁵And his ears were opened, and the ligament of his tongue was loosened and he spoke clearly. ³⁶And Jesus ordered them to tell no one about it, but the more he insisted, the more widely they published it. ³⁷Their admiration was unbounded. 'He has done all things well,' they said 'he makes the deaf hear and the dumb speak.'

Second miracle of the loaves

8 ¹And now once again a great crowd had gathered, and they had nothing to eat. So he called his disciples to him and said to them, ²'I feel sorry for all these people; they have been with me for three days now and have nothing to eat. ³If I send them off home hungry they will collapse on the way; some have come a great distance.' ⁴His disciples replied, 'Where could anyone get bread to feed these people in a deserted place like this?' ⁵He asked them, 'How many loaves have you?' 'Seven' they said. ⁶Then he instructed the crowd to sit down on the ground, and he took the seven loaves, and after giving thanks he broke them and handed them to his disciples to distribute; and they distributed them among the crowd. ⁷They had a few small fish as well, and over these he said a blessing and ordered them to be distributed also. ⁸They ate as much as they wanted, and they collected seven basketfuls of the scraps left over. ⁹Now there had been about four thousand people. He sent them away ¹⁰and immediately, getting into the boat with his disciples, went to the region of Dalmanutha.

The Pharisees ask for a sign from heaven

¹¹The Pharisees came up and started a discussion with him; they demanded of him a sign from heaven, to test him. ¹²And with a sigh that came straight from the heart he said, 'Why does this generation demand a sign? I tell you solemnly, no sign shall be given to this generation.' ¹³And leaving them again and re-embarking he went away to the opposite shore.

The yeast of the Pharisees and of Herod

[14]The disciples had forgotten to take any food and they had only one loaf with them in the boat. [15]Then he gave them this warning, 'Keep your eyes open; be on your guard against the yeast of the Pharisees and the yeast of Herod'. [16]And they said to one another, 'It is because we have no bread'. [17]And Jesus knew it, and he said to them, 'Why are you talking about having no bread? Do you not yet understand? Have you no perception? Are your minds closed? [18]Have you *eyes that do not see, ears that do not hear?*[a] Or do you not remember? [19]When I broke the five loaves among the five thousand, how many baskets full of scraps did you collect?' They answered, 'Twelve'. [20]And when I broke the seven loaves for the four thousand, how many baskets full of scraps did you collect?' And they answered, 'Seven'. [21]Then he said to them, 'Are you still without perception?'

Cure of a blind man at Bethsaida

[22]They came to Bethsaida, and some people brought to him a blind man whom they begged him to touch. [23]He took the blind man by the hand and led him outside the village. Then putting spittle on his eyes and laying his hands on him, he asked, 'Can you see anything?' [24]The man, who was beginning to see, replied, 'I can see people; they look like trees to me, but they are walking about'. [25]Then he laid his hands on the man's eyes again

---

[8] a. Jr 5:21; Ezk 12:2

and he saw clearly; he was cured, and he could see everything plainly and distinctly. ²⁶And Jesus sent him home, saying, 'Do not even go into the village'.

Peter's profession of faith

²⁷Jesus and his disciples left for the villages round Caesarea Philippi. On the way he put this question to his disciples, 'Who do people say I am?' ²⁸And they told him. 'John the Baptist,' they said 'others Elijah; others again, one of the prophets.' ²⁹'But you,' he asked 'who do you say I am?' Peter spoke up and said to him, 'You are the Christ'. ³⁰And he gave them strict orders not to tell anyone about him.

First prophecy of the Passion

³¹And he began to teach them that the Son of Man was destined to suffer grievously, to be rejected by the elders and the chief priests and the scribes, and to be put to death, and after three days to rise again; ³²and he said all this quite openly. Then, taking him aside, Peter started to remonstrate with him. ³³But, turning and seeing his disciples, he rebuked Peter and said to him, 'Get behind me, Satan! Because the way you think is not God's way but man's.'

The condition of following Christ

³⁴He called the people and his disciples to him and said, 'If anyone wants to be a follower of mine, let him renounce himself and take up his cross and follow me. ³⁵For anyone who wants to save his life will lose it; but anyone who loses his life for my sake, and for the sake of the gospel, will save

it. [36]What gain, then, is it for a man to win the whole world and ruin his life? [37]And indeed what can a man offer in exchange for his life? [38]For if anyone in this adulterous and sinful generation is ashamed of me and of my words, the Son of Man will also be ashamed of him when he comes in the glory of his Father with the holy angels.'

9 [1]And he said to them, 'I tell you solemnly, there are some standing here who will not taste death before they see the kingdom of God come with power'.

The transfiguration

[2]Six days later, Jesus took with him Peter and James and John and led them up a high mountain where they could be alone by themselves. There in their presence he was transfigured: [3]his clothes became dazzlingly white, whiter than any earthly bleacher could make them. [4]Elijah appeared to them with Moses; and they were talking with Jesus. [5]Then Peter spoke to Jesus: 'Rabbi,' he said 'it is wonderful for us to be here; so let us make three tents, one for you, one for Moses and one for Elijah'. [6]He did not know what to say; they were so frightened. [7]And a cloud came, covering them in shadow; and there came a voice from the cloud, 'This is my Son, the Beloved. Listen to him.' [8]Then suddenly, when they looked round, they saw no one with them any more but only Jesus.

The question about Elijah

[9]As they came down from the mountain he warned them to tell no one what they had seen, until after the Son of

Man had risen from the dead. [10]They observed the warning faithfully, though among themselves they discussed what 'rising from the dead' could mean. [11]And they put this question to him, 'Why do the scribes say that Elijah has to come first?' [12]'True,' he said 'Elijah is to come first and to see that everything is as it should be; yet how is it that the scriptures say about the Son of Man that he is to suffer grievously and be treated with contempt? [13]However, I tell you that Elijah has come and they have treated him as they pleased, just as the scriptures say about him.'

The epileptic demoniac

[14]When they rejoined the disciples they saw a large crowd round them and some scribes arguing with them. [15]The moment they saw him the whole crowd were struck with amazement and ran to greet him. [16]'What are you arguing about with them?' he asked. [17]A man answered him from the crowd, 'Master, I have brought my son to you; there is a spirit of dumbness in him, [18]and when it takes hold of him it throws him to the ground, and he foams at the mouth and grinds his teeth and goes rigid. And I asked your disciples to cast it out and they were unable to.' [19]'You faithless generation' he said to them in reply. 'How much longer must I be with you? How much longer must I put up with you? Bring him to me.' [20]They brought the boy to him, and as soon as the spirit saw Jesus it threw the boy into convulsions, and he fell to the ground and lay writhing

there, foaming at the mouth. [21]Jesus asked the father, 'How long has this been happening to him?' 'From childhood,' he replied [22]'and it has often thrown him into the fire and into the water, in order to destroy him. But if you can do anything, have pity on us and help us.' [23]'If you can?' retorted Jesus. 'Everything is possible for anyone who has faith.' [24]Immediately the father of the boy cried out, 'I do have faith. Help the little faith I have!' [25]And when Jesus saw how many people were pressing round him, he rebuked the unclean spirit. 'Deaf and dumb spirit,' he said 'I command you: come out of him and never enter him again.' [26]Then throwing the boy into violent convulsions it came out shouting, and the boy lay there so like a corpse that most of them said, 'He is dead'. [27]But Jesus took him by the hand and helped him up, and he was able to stand. [28]When he had gone indoors his disciples asked him privately, 'Why were we unable to cast it out?' [29]'This is the kind' he answered 'that can only be driven out by prayer.'

Second prophecy of the Passion

[30]After leaving that place they made their way through Galilee; and he did not want anyone to know, [31]because he was instructing his disciples; he was telling them, 'The Son of Man will be delivered into the hands of men; they will put him to death; and three days after he has been put to death he will rise again'. [32]But they did not understand what he said and were afraid to ask him.

Who is the greatest?

³³They came to Capernaum, and when he was in the house he asked them, 'What were you arguing about on the road?' ³⁴They said nothing because they had been arguing which of them was the greatest. ³⁵So he sat down, called the Twelve to him and said, 'If anyone wants to be first, he must make himself last of all and servant of all'. ³⁶He then took a little child, set him in front of them, put his arms round him, and said to them, ³⁷'Anyone who welcomes one of these little children in my name, welcomes me; and anyone who welcomes me welcomes not me but the one who sent me'.

On using the name of Jesus

³⁸John said to him, 'Master, we saw a man who is not one of us casting out devils in your name; and because he was not one of us we tried to stop him'. ³⁹But Jesus said, 'You must not stop him: no one who works a miracle in my name is likely to speak evil of me. ⁴⁰Anyone who is not against us is for us.

Charity shown to Christ's disciples

⁴¹'If anyone gives you a cup of water to drink just because you belong to Christ, then I tell you solemnly, he will most certainly not lose his reward.

On leading others astray

⁴²'But anyone who is an obstacle to bring down one of these little ones who have faith, would be better

thrown into the sea with a great millstone round his neck. [43]And if your hand should cause you to sin, cut it off; it is better for you to enter into life crippled, than to have two hands and go to hell, into the fire that cannot be put out. [45]And if your foot should cause you to sin, cut it off; it is better for you to enter into life lame, than to have two feet and be thrown into hell. [47]And if your eye should cause you to sin, tear it out; it is better for you to enter into the kingdom of God with one eye, than to have two eyes and be thrown into hell [48]where *their worm does not die nor their fire go out.*[a] [49]For everyone will be salted with fire. [50]Salt is a good thing, but if salt has become insipid, how can you season it again? Have salt in yourselves and be at peace with one another.'

The question about divorce

10 [1]Leaving there, he came to the district of Judaea and the far side of the Jordan. And again crowds gathered round him, and again he taught them, as his custom was. [2]Some Pharisees approached him and asked, 'Is it against the law for a man to divorce his wife?' They were testing him. [3]He answered them, 'What did Moses command you?' [4]'Moses allowed us' they said 'to draw up a writ of dismissal and so to divorce.' [5]Then Jesus said to them, 'It was because you were so unteachable that he

[9 a.] Is 66:24

wrote this commandment for you. ⁶But from the beginning of creation *God made them male and female.* ⁷*This is why a man must leave father and mother,* ⁸*and the two become one body.*ᵃ They are no longer two, therefore, but one body. ⁹So then, what God has united, man must not divide.' ¹⁰Back in the house the disciples questioned him again about this, ¹¹and he said to them, 'The man who divorces his wife and marries another is guilty of adultery against her. ¹²And if a woman divorces her husband and marries another she is guilty of adultery too.'

Jesus and the children

¹³People were bringing little children to him, for him to touch them. The disciples turned them away, ¹⁴but when Jesus saw this he was indignant and said to them, 'Let the little children come to me; do not stop them; for it is to such as these that the kingdom of God belongs. ¹⁵I tell you solemnly, anyone who does not welcome the kingdom of God like a little child will never enter it.' ¹⁶Then he put his arms round them, laid his hands on them and gave them his blessing.

The rich young man

¹⁷He was setting out on a journey when a man ran up, knelt before him and put this question to him, 'Good master, what must I do to inherit eternal life?' ¹⁸Jesus said to him,

---

ᵃ Gn 1:27; 2:24

'Why do you call me good? No one is good but God alone. [19]You know the commandments: *You must not kill; You must not commit adultery; You must not steal; You must not bring false witness;* You must not defraud; *Honour your father and mother.*' [20]And he said to him, 'Master, I have kept all these from my earliest days'. [21]Jesus looked steadily at him and loved him, and he said, 'There is one thing you lack. Go and sell everything you own and give the money to the poor, and you will have treasure in heaven; then come, follow me.' [22]But his face fell at these words and he went away sad, for he was a man of great wealth.

The danger of riches

[23]Jesus looked round and said to his disciples, 'How hard it is for those who have riches to enter the kingdom of God!' [24]The disciples were astounded by these words, but Jesus insisted, 'My children,' he said to them 'how hard it is to enter the kingdom of God! [25]It is easier for a camel to pass through the eye of a needle than for a rich man to enter the kingdom of God.' [26]They were more astonished than ever. 'In that case' they said to one another 'who can be saved?' [27]Jesus gazed at them. 'For men' he said 'it is impossible, but not for God: because everything is possible for God.'

The reward of renunciation

[28]Peter took this up. 'What about us?' he asked him. 'We have left everything and followed you.' [29]Jesus said, 'I tell

you solemnly, there is no one who has left house, brothers, sisters, father, children or land for my sake and for the sake of the gospel ³⁰who will not be repaid a hundred times over, houses, brothers, sisters, mothers, children and land - not without persecutions - now in this present time and, in the world to come, eternal life. ³¹'Many who are first will be last, and the last first.'

Third prophecy of the Passion

³²They were on the road, going up to Jerusalem; Jesus was walking on ahead of them; they were in a daze, and those who followed were apprehensive. Once more taking the Twelve aside he began to tell them what was going to happen to him: ³³'Now we are going up to Jerusalem, and the Son of Man is about to be handed over to the chief priests and the scribes. They will condemn him to death and will hand him over to the pagans, ³⁴who will mock him and spit at him and scourge him and put him to death; and after three days he will rise again.'

The sons of Zebedee make their request

³⁵James and John, the sons of Zebedee, approached him. 'Master,' they said to him 'we want you to do us a favour.' ³⁶He said to them, 'What is it you want me to do for you?' ³⁷They said to him, 'Allow us to sit one at your right hand and the other at your left in your glory'. ³⁸'You do not know what you are asking' Jesus said to them. 'Can you drink the cup that I must drink, or be baptised

with the baptism with which I must be baptised?' [39]They replied, 'We can'. Jesus said to them, 'The cup that I must drink you shall drink, and with the baptism with which I must be baptised you shall be baptised, [40]but as for seats at my right hand or my left, these are not mine to grant; they belong to those to whom they have been allotted'.

Leadership with service

[41]When the other ten heard this they began to feel indignant with James and John, [42]so Jesus called them to him and said to them, 'You know that among the pagans their so-called rulers lord it over them, and their great men make their authority felt. [43]This is not to happen among you. No; anyone who wants to become great among you must be your servant, [44]and anyone who wants to be first among you must be slave to all. [45]For the Son of Man himself did not come to be served but to serve, and to give his life as a ransom for many.'

The blind man of Jericho

[46]They reached Jericho; and as he left Jericho with his disciples and a large crowd, Bartimaeus (that is, the son of Timaeus), a blind beggar, was sitting at the side of the road. [47]When he heard that it was Jesus of Nazareth, he began to shout and to say, 'Son of David, Jesus, have pity on me'. [48]And many of them scolded him and told him to keep quiet, but he only shouted all the louder, 'Son of David, have pity on me'. [49]Jesus stopped and said, 'Call him here'. So they called the blind man. 'Courage,' they said 'get up;

he is calling you.' ⁵⁰So throwing off his cloak, he jumped up and went to Jesus. ⁵¹Then Jesus spoke, 'What do you want me to do for you?' 'Rabbuni,'ᵇ the blind man said to him 'Master, let me see again.' ⁵²Jesus said to him, 'Go; your faith has saved you'. And immediately his sight returned and he followed him along the road.

IV. THE JERUSALEM MINISTRY

The Messiah enters Jerusalem

11 ¹When they were approaching Jerusalem, in sight of Bethphage and Bethany, close by the Mount of Olives, he sent two of his disciples ²and said to them, 'Go off to the village facing you, and as soon as you enter it you will find a tethered colt that no one has yet ridden. Untie it and bring it here. ³If anyone says to you, "What are you doing?" say, "The Master needs it and will send it back here directly".' ⁴They went off and found a colt tethered near a door in the open street. As they untied it, ⁵some men standing there said, 'What are you doing, untying that colt?' ⁶They gave the answer Jesus had told them, and the men let them go. ⁷Then they took the colt to Jesus and threw their cloaks on its back, and he sat on it. ⁸Many people spread their cloaks on the road, others greenery which they had cut in the fields. ⁹And those who went in front and those who followed were all shouting, *Hosanna! Blessings on him*

---

¹⁰ᵇ. Aramaic: 'My master'.

who comes in the name of the Lord![a] [10]Blessings on the coming kingdom of our father David! Hosanna in the highest heavens!' [11]He entered Jerusalem and went into the Temple. He looked all round him, but as it was now late, he went out to Bethany with the Twelve.

The barren fig tree

[12]Next day as they were leaving Bethany, he felt hungry. [13]Seeing a fig tree in leaf some distance away, he went to see if he could find any fruit on it, but when he came up to it he found nothing but leaves; for it was not the season for figs. [14]And he addressed the fig tree. 'May no one ever eat fruit from you again' he said. And his disciples heard him say this.

The expulsion of the dealers from the Temple

[15]So they reached Jerusalem and he went into the Temple and began driving out those who were selling and buying there; he upset the tables of the money changers and the chairs of those who were selling pigeons. [16]Nor would he allow anyone to carry anything through the Temple. [17]And he taught them and said, 'Does not scripture say: *My house will be called a house of prayer for all the peoples?*[b] But you have turned it into *a robbers' den.*'[c] [18]This came to the ears of the chief priests and the scribes, and they tried to

[11a.] Ps 118:22-23
[11b.] Is 56:7
[11c.] Jr 7:11

find some way of doing away with him; they were afraid of him because the people were carried away by his teaching. ¹⁹And when evening came he went out of the city.

The fig tree withered. Faith and prayer

²⁰Next morning, as they passed by, they saw the fig tree withered to the roots. ²¹Peter remembered. 'Look, Rabbi,' he said to Jesus 'the fig tree you cursed has withered away.' ²²Jesus answered, 'Have faith in God. ²³I tell you solemnly, if anyone says to this mountain, "Get up and throw yourself into the sea", with no hesitation in his heart but believing that what he says will happen, it will be done for him. ²⁴I tell you therefore: everything you ask and pray for, believe that you have it already, and it will be yours. ²⁵And when you stand in prayer, forgive whatever you have against anybody, so that your Father in heaven may forgive your failings too.'

The authority of Jesus is questioned

²⁷They came to Jerusalem again, and as Jesus was walking in the Temple, the chief priests and the scribes and the elders came to him, ²⁸and they said to him, 'What authority have you for acting like this? Or who gave you authority to do these things?' ²⁹Jesus said to them, 'I will ask you a question, only one; answer me and I will tell you my authority for acting like this. ³⁰John's baptism: did it come from heaven, or from man? Answer me that.' ³¹And they argued it out this way among themselves: 'If

we say from heaven, he will say, "Then why did you refuse to believe him?" [32]But dare we say from man?' - they had the people to fear, for everyone held that John was a real prophet. [33]So their reply to Jesus was, 'We do not know'. And Jesus said to them, 'Nor will I tell you my authority for acting like this'.

Parable of the wicked husbandmen

12 [1]He went on to speak to them in parables, 'A man planted a vineyard; he fenced it round, dug out a trough for the winepress and built a tower; then he leased it to tenants and went abroad. [2]When the time came, he sent a servant to the tenants to collect from them his share of the produce from the vineyard. [3]But they seized the man, thrashed him and sent him away empty-handed. [4]Next he sent another servant to them; him they beat about the head and treated shamefully. [5]And he sent another and him they killed; then a number of others, and they thrashed some and killed the rest. [6]He had still someone left: his beloved son. He sent him to them last of all. "They will respect my son" he said. [7]But those tenants said to each other, "This is the heir. Come on, let us kill him, and the inheritance will be ours." [8]So they seized him and killed him and threw him out of the vineyard. [9]Now what will the owner of the vineyard do? He will come and make an end of the tenants and give the vineyard to others. [10]Have you not read this text of scripture:

*It was the stone rejected by the builders
that became the keystone.
[11]This was the Lord's doing
and it is wonderful to see?[a]*

[12]And they would have liked to arrest him, because they realised that the parable was aimed at them, but they were afraid of the crowds. So they left him alone and went away.

On tribute to Caesar

[13]Next they sent to him some Pharisees and some Herodians to catch him out in what he said. [14]These came and said to him, 'Master, we know you are an honest man, that you are not afraid of anyone, because a man's rank means nothing to you, and that you teach the way of God in all honesty. Is it permissible to pay taxes to Caesar or not? Should we pay, yes or no?' [15]Seeing through their hypocrisy he said to them, 'Why do you set this trap for me? Hand me a denarius and let me see it.' [16]They handed him one and he said, 'Whose head is this? Whose name?' 'Caesar's' they told him. [17]Jesus said to them, 'Give back to Caesar what belongs to Caesar - and to God what belongs to God'. This reply took them completely by surprise.

The resurrection of the dead

[18]Then some Sadducees - who deny that there is a resurrection - came to him and they put this question to

---

[12a.] Ps 118:22-23

him, [19]'Master, we have it from Moses in writing, if a man's brother dies leaving a wife but no child, the man must marry the widow to raise up children for his brother. [20]Now there were seven brothers. The first married a wife and then died leaving no children. [21]The second married the widow, and he too died leaving no children; with the third it was the same, [22]and none of the seven left any children. Last of all the woman herself died. [23]Now at the resurrection, when they rise again, whose wife will she be, since she had been married to all seven?' [24]Jesus said to them, 'Is not the reason why you go wrong, that you understand neither the scriptures nor the power of God? [25]For when they rise from the dead, men and women do not marry; no, they are like the angels in heaven. [26]Now about the dead rising again, have you never read in the Book of Moses, in the passage about the Bush, how God spoke to him and said: *I am the God of Abraham, the God of Isaac and the God of Jacob?*[b] [27]He is God, not of the dead, but of the living. You are very much mistaken.'

The greatest commandment of all

[28]One of the scribes who had listened to them debating and had observed how well Jesus had answered them, now came up and put a question to him, 'Which is the first of all the commandments?' [29]Jesus replied, 'This is the first: *Listen, Israel, the Lord our God is the one Lord,*

---

12 b. Ex 3:6

[30]*and you must love the Lord your God with all your heart, with all your soul*, with all your mind and *with all your strength.*[c] [31]The second is this: *You must love your neighbour as yourself.*[d] There is no commandment greater than these.' [32]The scribe said to him, 'Well spoken, Master; what you have said is true: that he is one and there is no other. [33]To love him with all your heart, with all your understanding and strength, and to love your neighbour as yourself, this is far more important than any holocaust or sacrifice.' [34]Jesus, seeing how wisely he had spoken, said, 'You are not far from the kingdom of God'. And after that no one dared to question him any more.

Christ not only son but also Lord of David

[35]Later, while teaching in the Temple, Jesus said, 'How can the scribes maintain that the Christ is the son of David? [36]David himself, moved by the Holy Spirit, said:

The Lord said to my Lord:
Sit at my right hand
and I will put your enemies
under your feet.[e]

[37]David himself calls him Lord, in what way then can he be his son?' And the great majority of the people heard this with delight.

[12 c.] Dt 6:4-5
[12 d.] Lv 19:18
[12 e.] Ps 110:1

The scribes condemned by Jesus

[38]In his teaching he said, 'Beware of the scribes who like to walk about in long robes, to be greeted obsequiously in the market squares, [39]to take the front seats in the synagogues and the places of honour at banquets; [40]these are the men who swallow the property of widows, while making a show of lengthy prayers. The more severe will be the sentence they receive.'

The widow's mite

[41]He sat down opposite the treasury and watched the people putting money into the treasury, and many of the rich put in a great deal. [42]A poor widow came and put in two small coins, the equivalent of a penny. [43]Then he called his disciples and said to them, 'I tell you solemnly, this poor widow has put more in than all who have contributed to the treasury; [44]for they have all put in money they had over, but she from the little she had has put in everything she possessed, all she had to live on'.

The eschatological discourse: introduction

13 [1]As he was leaving the Temple one of his disciples said to him, 'Look at the size of those stones, Master! Look at the size of those buildings!' [2]And Jesus said to him, 'You see these great buildings? Not a single stone will be left on another: everything will be destroyed.' [3]And while he was sitting facing the Temple, on the Mount of Olives, Peter, James, John and

Andrew questioned him privately, 4'Tell us, when is this going to happen, and what sign will there be that all this is about to be fulfilled?'

The beginning of sorrows

5Then Jesus began to tell them, 'Take care that no one deceives you. 6Many will come using my name and saying, "I am he", and they will deceive many. 7When you hear of wars and rumours of wars, do not be alarmed, this is something that must happen, but the end will not be yet. 8For nation will fight against nation, and kingdom against kingdom. There will be earthquakes here and there; there will be famines. This is the beginning of the birthpangs. 9Be on your guard: they will hand you over to sanhedrins; you will be beaten in synagogues; and you will stand before governors and kings for my sake, to bear witness before them, 10since the Good News must first be proclaimed to all the nations. 11And when they lead you away to hand you over, do not worry beforehand about what to say; no, say whatever is given to you when the time comes, because it is not you who will be speaking: it will be the Holy Spirit. 12Brother will betray brother to death, and the father his child; children will rise against their parents and have them put to death. 13You will be hated by all men on account of my name; but the man who stands firm to the end will be saved.

The great tribulation of Jerusalem

[14]'When you see *the disastrous abomination*[a] set up where it ought not to be (let the reader understand), then those in Judaea must escape to the mountains; [15]if a man is on the housetop, he must not come down to go into the house to collect any of his belongings; [16]if a man is in the fields, he must not turn back to fetch his cloak. [17]Alas for those with child, or with babies at the breast, when those days come! [18]Pray that this may not be in winter. [19]For in those days there will be *such distress as, until now, has not been*[b] equalled since the beginning when God created the world, nor ever will be again. [20]And if the Lord had not shortened that time, no one would have survived; but he did shorten the time, for the sake of the elect whom he chose. [21]And if anyone says to you then, "Look, here is the Christ" or, "Look, he is there", do not believe it; [22]for false Christs and false prophets will arise and produce signs and portents to deceive the elect, if that were possible. [23]You therefore must be on your guard. I have forewarned you of everything.

The coming of the Son of Man

[24]'But in those days, after that time of distress, the sun will be darkened, the moon will lose its brightness, [25]the stars will come falling from heaven and the powers in

---

[13a.] Dn 9:27, and ch. 11, 12
[13b.] Dn 12:1

the heavens will be shaken. ²⁶And then they will see the Son of Man coming in the clouds with great power and glory; ²⁷then too he will send the angels to gather his chosen from the four winds, from the ends of the world to the ends of heaven.

The time of this coming

²⁸'Take the fig tree as a parable: as soon as its twigs grow supple and its leaves come out, you know that summer is near. ²⁹So with you when you see these things happening: know that he is near, at the very gates. ³⁰I tell you solemnly, before this generation has passed away all these things will have taken place. ³¹Heaven and earth will pass away, but my words will not pass away. ³²But as for that day or hour, nobody knows it, neither the angels of heaven, nor the Son; no one but the Father.

Be on the alert

³³'Be on your guard, stay awake, because you never know when the time will come. ³⁴It is like a man travelling abroad: he has gone from home, and left his servants in charge, each with his own task; and he has told the doorkeeper to stay awake. ³⁵So stay awake, because you do not know when the master of the house is coming, evening, midnight, cockcrow, dawn; ³⁶if he comes unexpectedly, he must not find you asleep. ³⁷And what I say to you I say to all: Stay awake!'

V. PASSION AND RESURRECTION

The conspiracy against Jesus

14 [1]It was two days before the Passover and the feast of Unleavened Bread, and the chief priests and the scribes were looking for a way to arrest Jesus by some trick and have him put to death. [2]For they said, 'It must not be during the festivities, or there will be a disturbance among the people'.

The anointing at Bethany

[3]Jesus was at Bethany in the house of Simon the leper; he was at dinner when a woman came in with an alabaster jar of very costly ointment, pure nard. She broke the jar and poured the ointment on his head. [4]Some who were there said to one another indignantly, 'Why this waste of ointment? [5]Ointment like this could have been sold for over three hundred denarii and the money given to the poor'; and they were angry with her. [6]But Jesus said, 'Leave her alone. Why are you upsetting her? What she has done for me is one of the good works. [7]You have the poor with you always, and you can be kind to them whenever you wish, but you will not always have me. [8]She has done what was in her power to do: she has anointed my body beforehand for its burial. [9]I tell you solemnly, wherever throughout all the world the Good News is proclaimed, what she has done will be told also, in remembrance of her.'

Judas betrays Jesus

[10]Judas Iscariot, one of the Twelve, approached the chief priests with an offer to hand Jesus over to them. [11]They were delighted to hear it, and promised to give him money; and he looked for a way of betraying him when the opportunity should occur.

Preparations for the Passover supper

[12]On the first day of Unleavened Bread, when the Passover lamb was sacrificed, his disciples said to him, 'Where do you want us to go and make the preparations for you to eat the passover?' [13]So he sent two of his disciples, saying to them, 'Go into the city and you will meet a man carrying a pitcher of water. Follow him, [14]and say to the owner of the house which he enters, "The Master says: Where is my dining room in which I can eat the passover with my disciples?" [15]He will show you a large upper room furnished with couches, all prepared. Make the preparations for us there.' [16]The disciples set out and went to the city and found everything as he had told them, and prepared the Passover.

The treachery of Judas foretold

[17]When evening came he arrived with the Twelve. [18]And while they were at table eating, Jesus said, 'I tell you solemnly, one of you is about to betray me, one of you eating with me'. [19]They were distressed and asked him, one after another, 'Not I, surely?' [20]He said to them, 'It is one of

the Twelve, one who is dipping into the same dish with me. [21]Yes, the Son of Man is going to his fate, as the scriptures say he will, but alas for that man by whom the Son of Man is betrayed! Better for that man if he had never been born!'

The institution of the Eucharist

[22]And as they were eating he took some bread, and when he had said the blessing he broke it and gave it to them. 'Take it,' he said 'this is my body.' [23]Then he took a cup, and when he had returned thanks he gave it to them, and all drank from it, [24]and he said to them, 'This is my blood, the blood of the covenant, which is to be poured out for many. [25]I tell you solemnly, I shall not drink any more wine until the day I drink the new wine in the kingdom of God.'

Peter's denial foretold

[26]After psalms had been sung they left for the Mount of Olives. [27]And Jesus said to them, 'You will all lose faith, for the scripture says: *I shall strike the shepherd and the sheep will be scattered,*[a] [28]however after my resurrection I shall go before you to Galilee'. [29]Peter said, 'Even if all lose faith, I will not'. [30]And Jesus said to him, 'I tell you solemnly, this day, this very night, before the cock crows twice, you will have disowned me three times'. [31]But he repeated still more earnestly, 'If I have to die with you, I will never disown you'. And they all said the same.

[14 a.] Zc 13:7

Gethsemane

[32]They came to a small estate called Gethsemane, and Jesus said to his disciples, 'Stay here while I pray'. [33]Then he took Peter and James and John with him. And a sudden fear came over him, and great distress. [34]And he said to them, 'My soul is sorrowful to the point of death. Wait here, and keep awake.' [35]And going on a little further he threw himself on the ground and prayed that, if it were possible, this hour might pass him by. [36]'Abba (Father)!' he said 'Everything is possible for you. Take this cup away from me. But let it be as you, not I, would have it.' [37]He came back and found them sleeping, and he said to Peter, 'Simon, are you asleep? Had you not the strength to keep awake one hour? [38]You should be awake, and praying not to be put to the test. The spirit is willing, but the flesh is weak.' [39]Again he went away and prayed, saying the same words. [40]And once more he came back and found them sleeping, their eyes were so heavy; and they could find no answer for him. [41]He came back a third time and said to them, 'You can sleep on now and take your rest. It is all over. The hour has come. Now the Son of Man is to be betrayed into the hands of sinners. [42]Get up! Let us go! My betrayer is close at hand already.'

The arrest

[43]Even while he was still speaking, Judas, one of the Twelve, came up with a number of men armed with

swords and clubs, sent by the chief priests and the scribes and the elders. ⁴⁴Now the traitor had arranged a signal with them. 'The one I kiss,' he had said 'he is the man. Take him in charge, and see he is well guarded when you lead him away.' ⁴⁵So when the traitor came, he went straight up to Jesus and said, 'Rabbi!' and kissed him. ⁴⁶The others seized him and took him in charge. ⁴⁷Then one of the bystanders drew his sword and struck out at the high priest's servant, and cut off his ear. ⁴⁸Then Jesus spoke. 'Am I a brigand' he said 'that you had to set out to capture me with swords and clubs? ⁴⁹I was among you teaching in the Temple day after day and you never laid hands on me. But this is to fulfil the scriptures.' ⁵⁰And they all deserted him and ran away. ⁵¹A young man who followed him had nothing on but a linen cloth. They caught hold of him, ⁵²but he left the cloth in their hands and ran away naked.

Jesus before the Sanhedrin

⁵³They led Jesus off to the high priest; and all the chief priests and the elders and the scribes assembled there. ⁵⁴Peter had followed him at a distance, right into the high priest's palace, and was sitting with the attendants warming himself at the fire. ⁵⁵The chief priests and the whole Sanhedrin were looking for evidence against Jesus on which they might pass the death-sentence. But they could not find any. ⁵⁶Several, indeed, brought false

evidence against him, but their evidence was conflicting.
[57]Some stood up and submitted this false evidence
against him, [58]'We heard him say, "I am going to destroy
this Temple made by human hands, and in three days
build another, not made by human hands"'. [59]But even on
this point their evidence was conflicting. [60]The high
priest then stood up before the whole assembly and put
this question to Jesus, 'Have you no answer to that?
What is this evidence these men are bringing against
you?' [61]But he was silent and made no answer at all. The
high priest put a second question to him, 'Are you the
Christ,' he said 'the Son of the Blessed One?' [62]'I am,'
said Jesus 'and you will see *the Son of Man seated at the
right hand of the Power and coming with the clouds of
heaven.'*[b] [63]The high priest tore his robes, 'What need of
witnesses have we now?' he said. [64]'You heard the
blasphemy. What is your finding?' And they all gave
their verdict: he deserved to die. [65]Some of them started
spitting at him and, blindfolding him, began hitting him
with their fists and shouting, 'Play the prophet!' And the
attendants rained blows on him.

Peter's denials

[66]While Peter was down below in the courtyard, one of
the high priest's servant-girls came up. [67]She saw Peter
warming himself there, stared at him and said, 'You too

[14b]. Dn 7:13; Ps 110:1

were with Jesus, the man from Nazareth'. ⁶⁸But he denied it. 'I do not know, I do not understand, what you are talking about' he said. And he went out into the forecourt. ⁶⁹The servant-girl saw him and again started telling the bystanders, 'This fellow is one of them'. ⁷⁰But again he denied it. A little later the bystanders themselves said to Peter, 'You are one of them for sure! Why, you are a Galilean.' ⁷¹But he started calling down curses on himself and swearing, 'I do not know the man you speak of'. ⁷²At that moment the cock crew for the second time, and Peter recalled how Jesus had said to him, 'Before the cock crows twice, you will have disowned me three times'. And he burst into tears.

Jesus before Pilate

15 ¹First thing in the morning, the chief priests together with the elders and scribes, in short the whole Sanhedrin, had their plan ready. They had Jesus bound and took him away and handed him over to Pilate. ²Pilate questioned him, 'Are you the king of the Jews?' 'It is you who say it' he answered. ³And the chief priests brought many accusations against him. Pilate questioned him again, 'Have you no reply at all? See how many accusations they are bringing against you!' ⁵But, to Pilate's amazement, Jesus made no further reply. ⁶At festival time Pilate used to release a prisoner for them, anyone they asked for. ⁷Now a man called

Barabbas was then in prison with the rioters who had committed murder during the uprising. [8]When the crowd went up and began to ask Pilate the customary favour, [9]Pilate answered them, 'Do you want me to release for you the king of the Jews?' [10]For he realised it was out of jealousy that the chief priests had handed Jesus over. [11]The chief priests, however, had incited the crowd to demand that he should release Barabbas for them instead. [12]Then Pilate spoke again. 'But in that case,' he said to them 'what am I to do with the man you call king of the Jews?' [13]They shouted back, 'Crucify him!' [14]'Why?' Pilate asked them 'What harm has he done?' But they shouted all the louder, 'Crucify him!' [15]So Pilate, anxious to placate the crowd, released Barabbas for them and, having ordered Jesus to be scourged, handed him over to be crucified.

Jesus crowned with thorns

[16]The soldiers led him away to the inner part of the palace, that is, the Praetorium, and called the whole cohort together. [17]They dressed him up in purple, twisted some thorns into a crown and put it on him. [18]And they began saluting him, 'Hail, king of the Jews!' [19]They struck his head with a reed and spat on him; and they went down on their knees to do him homage. [20]And when they had finished making fun of him, they took off the purple and dressed him in his own clothes.

The way of the cross

They led him out to crucify him. ²¹They enlisted a passer-by, Simon of Cyrene, father of Alexander and Rufus,ª who was coming in from the country, to carry his cross. ²²They brought Jesus to the place called Golgotha, which means the place of the skull.

The crucifixion

²³They offered him wine mixed with myrrh, but he refused it. ²⁴Then they crucified him, and shared out his clothing, casting lots to decide what each should get. ²⁵It was the third hourᵇ when they crucified him. ²⁶The inscription giving the charge against him read: 'The King of the Jews'. ²⁷And they crucified two robbers with him, one on his right and one on his left.

The crucified Christ is mocked

²⁹The passers-by jeered at him; they shook their heads and said, 'Aha! So you would destroy the Temple and rebuild it in three days! ³⁰Then save yourself: come down from the cross!' ³¹The chief priests and the scribes mocked him among themselves in the same way. 'He saved others,' they said 'he cannot save himself. ³²Let the Christ, the king of Israel, come down from the cross now, for us to see it and believe.' Even those who were crucified with him taunted him.

---

¹⁵ª. Alexander and Rufus were doubtless known to the Roman circle in which Mark wrote his gospel. Cf. Rm 16:13.
¹⁵ᵇ. 9 a.m.

The death of Jesus

[33]When the sixth hour came there was darkness over the whole land until the ninth hour. [34]And at the ninth hour Jesus cried out in a loud voice, 'Eloi, Eloi, lama sabachthani?' which means, *'My God, my God, why have you deserted me?'*[c] [35]When some of those who stood by heard this, they said, 'Listen, he is calling on Elijah'. [36]Someone ran and soaked a sponge in vinegar and, putting it on a reed, gave it him to drink saying; 'Wait and see if Elijah will come to take him down'. [37]But Jesus gave a loud cry and breathed his last. [38]And the veil of the Temple was torn in two from top to bottom. [39]The centurion, who was standing in front of him, had seen how he had died, and he said, 'In truth this man was a son of God'.

The women on Calvary

[40]There were some women watching from a distance. Among them were Mary of Magdala, Mary who was the mother of James the younger and Joset, and Salome. [41]These used to follow him and look after him when he was in Galilee. And there were many other women there who had come up to Jerusalem with him.

The burial

[42]It was now evening, and since it was Preparation Day (that is, the vigil of the sabbath), [43]there came Joseph of

---

[15 c] Ps 22:1

Arimathaea, a prominent member of the Council, who himself lived in the hope of seeing the kingdom of God, and he boldly went to Pilate and asked for the body of Jesus. ⁴⁴Pilate, astonished that he should have died so soon, summoned the centurion and enquired if he was already dead. ⁴⁵Having been assured of this by the centurion, he granted the corpse to Joseph ⁴⁶who bought a shroud, took Jesus down from the cross, wrapped him in the shroud and laid him in a tomb which had been hewn out of the rock. He then rolled a stone against the entrance to the tomb. ⁴⁷Mary of Magdala and Mary the mother of Joset were watching and took note of where he was laid.

The empty tomb. The angel's message

16 ¹When the sabbath was over, Mary of Magdala, Mary the mother of James, and Salome, bought spices with which to go and anoint him. ²And very early in the morning on the first day of the week they went to the tomb, just as the sun was rising. ³They had been saying to one another, 'Who will roll away the stone for us from the entrance to the tomb?' ⁴But when they looked they could see that the stone - which was very big - had already been rolled back. ⁵On entering the tomb they saw a young man in a white robe seated on the right-hand side, and they were struck with amazement. ⁶But he said to them, 'There is no need for alarm. You are looking for Jesus of Nazareth, who was crucified: he has risen, he is not here.

See, here is the place where they laid him. [7]But you must go and tell his disciples and Peter, "He is going before you to Galilee; it is there you will see him, just as he told you".' [8]And the women came out and ran away from the tomb because they were frightened out of their wits; and they said nothing to a soul, for they were afraid...

Appearances of the risen Christ[a]

[9]Having risen in the morning on the first day of the week, he appeared first to Mary of Magdala from whom he had cast out seven devils. [10]She then went to those who had been his companions, and who were mourning and in tears, and told them. [11]But they did not believe her when they heard her say that he was alive and that she had seen him. [12]After this, he showed himself under another form to two of them as they were on their way into the country. [13]These went back and told the others, who did not believe them either. [14]Lastly, he showed himself to the Eleven themselves while they were at table. He reproached them for their incredulity and obstinacy, because they had refused to believe those who had seen him after he had risen. [15]And he said to them, 'Go out to the whole world; proclaim the Good News to all creation. [16]He who believes and is baptised will be saved; he who does not believe will be condemned. [17]These are

---

[16a.] Many MSS omit vv. 9-20 and this ending to the gospel may not have been written by Mark, though it is old enough.

the signs that will be associated with believers: in my name they will cast out devils; they will have the gift of tongues; [18]they will pick up snakes in their hands, and be unharmed should they drink deadly poison; they will lay their hands on the sick, who will recover.' [19]And so the Lord Jesus, after he had spoken to them, was taken up into heaven: there at the right hand of God he took his place, [20]while they, going out, preached everywhere, the Lord working with them and confirming the word by the signs that accompanied it.

Informative Catholic Reading

We hope that you have enjoyed reading this booklet.

If you would like to find out more about CTS booklets - we'll send you our free information pack and catalogue.

Please send us your details:

    Name ....

    Address ....

    ....

    ....

    Postcode ....

    Telephone...

    Email ....

Send to: CTS, 40-46 Harleyford Road,
            Vauxhall, London
            SE11 5AY

Tel: 020 7640 0042
Fax: 020 7640 0046
Email: info@cts-online.org.uk